MW01701530

LEARN TO
IN
8
LESSONS OR LESS

Written by Bobby Broome

Saving Lives One Person At A Time

PLEASE ADHERE TO ALL OF THE SAFETY WARNINGS, LESSONS, AND SUGGESTIONS. BY DOING SO, YOU SHOULD HAVE SAFE AND EVENT FREE AQUATIC EXPERIENCES. PREVENTING ACCIDENTS SHOULD ALWAYS BE A PART OF EVERYONE'S THOUGHT PROCESS WHEN PARTICIPATING IN AQUATIC ACTIVITIES.

IN NO EVENT SHALL BOBBY BROOME AQUATICS PUBLISHING, IT'S DIRECTORS OFFICERS, SHAREHOLDERS, PARENTS, SUBSIDIARIES, AGENTS AND LICENSORS, OR CONTENT PROVIDERS BE LIABLE FOR ANY DIRECT, INDIRECT, SPECIAL (INCLUDING LOSS OF REVENUE OR INCOME, PAIN AND SUFFERING, EMOTIONAL DISTRESS, OR SIMILAR DAMAGES), INCIDENTAL, PUNITIVE, OR CONSEQUENTIAL DAMAGES ARISING OUT OF OR RELATED TO THE USE, INABILITY TO USE, AUTHORIZED USE, PERFORMANCE, OR NONPERFORMANCE OF THIS BOOK, EVEN IF BOBBY BROOME AQUATICS PUBLISHING WAS PREVIOUSLY ADVISED OF THE POSSIBILITY OF SUCH DAMAGES AND REGARDLESS OF WHETHER SUCH DAMAGES ARISE IN CONTRACT. TORT, UNDER STATUTE, IN EQUITY, AT LAW, OR OTHERWISE."

Copyright © 2009 Robert P. Broome

Library of Congress Catalog Card Number: Pending

All Rights Reserved: No part of this publication may be reproduced, stored in a retrieval system, or transmitted in any form or by any means, electronic, mechanical. Photocopying, recording, or otherwise, without prior written permission from the publisher.

Published by:
Bobby Broome Aquatics Publishing
bobbybroome@hotmail.com

ISBN 978-0-9771199-2-9

Table of contents

	Table of contents	i
Acknowledgements		v
Forward		vi
Sources		vii
Notes		viii
Chapter 1 – Introduction		**1**
Chapter 2 - Lesson 1		**5**
1	Tour the swimming area.	5
2	Sit down and review water safety rules.	6
3	Flutter kick - sitting on the side of the pool or near shore	6
4	Breathing - sitting on the side of the pool or near shore	7
5	Get in the water.	7
6	Get out of the water.	8
7	Get in the water, hold the wall or stand in water about waist to shoulder deep and get comfortable.	8
8	Holding breaths - blow bubbles with the mouth, nose and then the head in the water	9
9	Bobbing - with or without support	10
10	Holding breaths - submerge the mouth, nose, face or entire head and pick up toys	10
11	Flutter kick - on the front with support	11
12	Front glide - in the streamline position -with or without support and stand up	12
13	Front glide and flutter kick in the streamline position - with or without support	13
14	Front glide and flutter kick - with a kickboard - with or without support	13
15	Game	14
Chapter 3 - Lesson 2		**17**
1	Flutter kick - sitting on the side of the pool or near shore	17
2	Breathing - sitting on the side of the pool or near shore	17
3	Get in the water.	17
4	Holding breaths - blow bubbles with the mouth, nose and then the head in the water	17
5	Bobbing - with or without support	18
6	Front glide and flutter kick - with or without support	18
7	Front glide and flutter kick - with a kickboard - with or without support	18
8	Back float - with or without support and stand up	18
9	Back glide – with the arms at the side then stand up	20

10	Back glide and flutter kick - with or without support	21
11	Back glide and flutter kick - with kickboard -with or without support	21
12	Game	22
Chapter 4 - Lesson 3		**24**
1	Get in the water.	25
2	Bobbing	25
3	Holding breaths –underwater	25
4	Front glide and flutter kick - with a kickboard - with or without support	25
5	Front float	25
6	Back float	26
7	Back glide and flutter kick - with a kickboard - with or without support	26
8	Flutter kick on the back - with finning	26
9	Front crawl	27
10	Level off on the front and swim to safety.	29
11	Little jump - level off on the front and swim to the wall	30
12	Game	30
Chapter 5 - Lesson 4		**31**
1	Get in the water.	31
2	Bobbing	31
3	Bobbing - away from the wall or shore and back to safety	31
4	Holding breaths – underwater	32
5	Front float	32
6	Front glide and flutter kick - with a kickboard - with or without support	32
7	Back float	32
8	Back glide and flutter kick - with a kickboard - with or without support	32
9	Front crawl – with breathing - with or without assistance	32
10	Front crawl roll over and back float	34
11	Flutter kick on the back - with finning	35
12	Level off on the back and swim to safety.	35
13	Little jump - level off on the back and swim to the wall	35
14	Game	35
Chapter 6 - Lesson 5		**37**
1	Get in the water.	37

2	Front glide and flutter kick - with a kickboard - with or without assistance	37
3	Back glide and flutter kick - with a kickboard - with or without assistance	37
4	Front crawl – with breathing - with or without assistance	37
5	Flutter kick on the back - with finning	37
6	Front crawl rollover and back float	37
7	Big jump - swim back to the wall on front and back	37
8	Breaststroke kick -sitting on the side of the pool or near shore	38
9	Breaststroke kick on the back - with a kickboard - with or without assistance	38
10	Breaststroke kick - on the front - with a kickboard - with or without assistance	39
11	Game	40
Chapter 7 - Lesson 6		**41**
1	Jump in and swim back to the wall.	41
2	Front glide and flutter kick - with a kickboard - with or without assistance	41
3	Back glide and flutter kick - with a kickboard - with or without assistance	41
4	Back glide and breaststroke kick - with a kickboard - with or without assistance	41
5	Front glide and breaststroke kick - with a kickboard - with or without assistance	41
6	Front crawl - with breathing - with or without assistance	41
7	Flutter kick on the back -with finning	41
8	Front float rollover and back float then rollover and front float	42
9	Front crawl - rollover on the back and take one breath, then continue swimming on the front	42
10	Front crawl - roll on to the side and take one breath, then continue swimming on the front	43
11	Jellyfish Float	43
12	Survival Float	43
13	Game	44
Chapter 8 - Lesson 7		**45**
1	Jump in and swim back to the wall.	45
2	Front glide and flutter kick - with a kickboard - with or without assistance	45
3	Back glide and flutter kick - with a kickboard - with or without assistance	45
4	Back glide and breaststroke kick - with a kickboard - with or without assistance	45
5	Front glide and breaststroke kick - with a kickboard - with or without assistance	45
6	Front crawl - with breathing - with assistance	46

7	Flutter kick on the back - with finning	46
8	Front crawl - rollover on the back and take one breath, then continue swimming on the front	46
9	Front crawl - with rotary breathing	46
10	Elementary backstroke	47
11	Treading water	48
12	Game	50
Chapter 9 - Lesson 8		**51**
1	Jump in and swim back to the wall.	51
2	Front glide and flutter kick - with a kickboard - with or without assistance	51
3	Back glide and flutter kick - with a kickboard - with or without assistance	51
4	Back glide and breaststroke kick - with a kickboard - with or without assistance	51
5	Front glide and breaststroke kick - with a kickboard - with or without assistance	51
6	Front crawl - with rotary breathing	51
7	Flutter kick on the back - with finning	51
8	Elementary backstroke	51
9	Survival float	51
10	Treading water	51
11	Game	51

Acknowledgements:

Thank you God for your presence in my life. Thank you for blessing me with the understanding and drive necessary to produce this work.

This book is dedicated to my parents, Pershing and Delores M. Broome and my stepmother, Annette C. Broome.

Thank you my children, Jason Tyreese Gordon, Jermaine Claxton Gordon, and Bobbi Rozann Broome for your love and inspiration. Thank you Linda Turner for your support and help with Bobbi. I could not do it without you. To my brothers Richard and Michael, and my sister Kimberly, I love you all very much. Thank you, to all of my family and friends who have supported me, and challenged me. You have all inspired and pushed me forward.

Thank you, to all of the facilities that have employed me and allowed me to practice my craft:

- The American Red Cross National Headquarters in Washington DC
- Fort Meyers Military Community in Arlington, Virginia
- Lake Barcroft in Falls Church, Virginia
- California State University Dominguez Hills in Carson, California
- Lakeside Golf Club in Burbank, California
- The Hollywood Wilshire YMCA in Hollywood, California
- The East Valley YMCA in North Hollywood California
- California State University Long Beach in Long Beach, California
- Cerritos College Community Education Program in Cerritos, California
- Residential pool owners all around Los Angeles County

Reviews and comments were provided by, Bobbi Rozann Broome, Jean Conner and Lance Howden. Thank you for your valuable time and insight.

Thank you to Frank Davis of Faith Star Entertainment World Wide Incorporated for your friendship and support.

Thank you to Aurora Threats for your inspiration, love and support.

To each student that I have had the pleasure of teaching, this work is especially dedicated to you.

Foreword:

I wrote this book to share my tried and tested method of learning to swim in eight lessons or less. It has never taken more than eight lessons for me to teach anyone to swim with, the exception of a few people of the thousands of people that I have taught to swim because of mitigating circumstances. In most cases, my students learn in less than eight lessons.

For years, I could not understand why other instructors could not get consistent results as fast as I could and the instructors that I have mentored and trained. I have concluded that if instructors and learners focus on and emphasized the small details that make a big difference: breath control, relaxation and body position from the beginning and for every skill, learning to swim can be accomplished quickly and with ease. It sounds simple because it simple.

Many instructors are less focused on the small details, they introduce and allow learners to practice bad habits and they often use swim team drills to teach beginners. By practicing good swimming habits and following the instructions in this program, learning to swim can and will be accomplished with relative ease, even if it takes a few more than eight lessons.

This book was written for those people who prefer to get right to the point. Many books, including my last book, "The Parent's Guide To: Water Safety And Swim Instruction" include extensive detail that some people may not have the patience or time to read. "Learn to Swim in 8 Lessons or Less" is as easy of a read as it is to learn to swim using the program. The instructions are easy to follow and if a visual reference is needed, refer to the corresponding DVD available in winter 2010 or "The Parent's Guide To: Water Safety And Swim Instruction" which includes full color pictures.

The best way to prevent drowning is to follow water safety rules and learn to swim. I feel like each time I teach someone to swim that I am saving a life. This is my God given gift. Thank you for allowing me to share my gift.

God Bless You,

Bobby Broome
Saving Lives One Person At A Time

Sources

- Water Safety Instructor's Manual (The American Red Cross Revised 2009)
- The Parent's Guide To: Water Safety And Swim Instruction (Robert P. Broome 2005)
- Steven J. Langendorfer's and Lawrence D. Bruya's (Aquatic Readiness 1995)
- Every person that I have had the pleasure of teaching.

Notes:

Chapter 1 - Introduction

Learning to swim is the best way to prevent death by unintentional drowning. It does not guarantee that a person will not drown, but knowing how to swim certainly increases the chances of survival. Swimming is a life-long skill that promotes good health, good work ethic and self-confidence. Whether swimming in a pool, lake, ocean, river or creek, use this book to teach yourself or someone else to swim in eight easy lessons or less. Learners should practice at least one lesson per week. For best results, practice two to four lessons per week. It is possible to learn to swim in as few as two weeks. Prepare for each lesson by reviewing the lesson plans before entering the swimming area. Take note of the good habit tips and the practice tips associated with the lessons before and after the skills charts. These tips are helpful and add clarity to the learning process.

Anyone who wants to learn how to swim can successfully learn by applying the necessary effort. This book details a step-by-step method for learning or teaching someone about three years old or older to swim in approximately eight, 30 to 45 minute lessons. Each lesson teaches water safety habits and swimming skills using easy progressions. The skills are arranged in a systematic order designed to prepare learners for each next step. Learners practice easier skills before trying skills that are more difficult. Each skill is presented with detailed instructions. The instructions are easy to follow for most people. However, because people learn differently, depending on developmental age, cognitive capacity and physical ability, it is important to comprehend the mechanics of the skills and use individual creativity to learn or teach the skills.

Using the methodology in this book, the expected level of proficiency is subjective. The author's intent is for beginners to learn breath control, the ability to relax and propulsion of the body a reasonable distance. The goal is to make swimming, and learning to swim, easy and pleasant. Learners will develop good swimming and water safety habits. Some learners will achieve this minimum standard; others will exceed expectations because of mastering these basic skills quickly and become reasonably strong swimmers within the eight lessons. The level of proficiency primarily depends on the learners' initial level of fear of the water. With practice, persistence and following the progressions of the skills as outlined, learners can overcome their fear of the water. Practice skills as long as necessary until they can be perform them with confidence and relative ease, then add new skills to the routine. The design of the lessons allows ample time to learn the skills with proficiency. Learners who catch on faster may move ahead to skills in following lessons. Fearful or less coordinated learners, due to maturity or physical limitations, can work on the skills within the first four lessons throughout the eight-lesson program. There are enough skills within the first four lessons to work on and learn to swim with reasonable proficiency in shallow water. Learners who catch on quickly will be able to advance to the skills in the last four lessons, become stronger swimmers and swim comfortably in deep water.

Additional practice after the eight-lesson program will result in stronger and improved swimming ability. Preschool age children, ages three to five or six years old should be able to achieve breath control, relaxing and propulsion on the front and back using good body position within eight lessons. However, since preschoolers, are generally not as strong and less coordinated; their skills may not look as smooth and may take longer to master than older learners. Learners should practice the basic skills in Lessons 1 and 2 until they are comfortable before adding the more difficult skills. The lesson design incorporates a routine of continued practice of the basic skills throughout the eight-lesson program. People who are slow to learn the skills in the first two lessons will eventually break through their fear or coordination barrier and catch up.

The progressions of skills throughout the eight lessons are based on the learning ability of more apprehensive and fearful learners. When learning and teaching each skill, it is important to focus on the three basic swimming habits that are important for all swimmers, beginners to experts: breath control, relaxation and body position. By doing so, learning to swim will be easier, faster and more enjoyable.

Be patient and stick to the routine. The time spent and number of repetitions practiced on each skill will depend on the learners' level of proficiency, endurance and attention span. Develop a routine that starts with the skills practiced and learned in previous lessons. Then practice a new skill or two and add them to the routine in the next lesson. Use toys and play games that enhance learning. End each lesson with at least five minutes of fun and games. As skills are mastered, either decrease repetitions or stop practicing those skills to make room in the routine for new skills or more repetitions of skills still needing improvement. Celebrate each accomplishment no matter how small or large.

Approach learning and teaching in a few different ways. If you are using this book to teach yourself to swim, you probably have the cognitive ability to follow directions as written. Therefore, you should achieve the desired result. If you are using this book to teach someone else, the following are teaching methods you may use: "explain, demonstrate, practice and help" or "guided discovery." Explain, demonstrate, practice and help is explained in detail in Bobby Broome's "The Parent's Guide To: Water Safety And Swim Instruction" 2005. Guided discovery is explained in detail in Steven J. Langendorfer's and Lawrence D. Bruya's Aquatic Readiness 1995. Both of these methods are explained in detail in the American Red Cross "Water Safety Instructor's Manual" 2009. These two methods provide you with a solid teaching foundation. Feel free to expand on these methods in your own creative way. There is no one perfect method for every learner. Learners are unique unto themselves.

Explain, demonstrate, practice and help works well for learners about six years old and older. Explain the skill, demonstrate the skill and allow learners to try and then practice the skill. To help learners:

- Assist them by providing support or assistance as learners try to perform the skill.
- Physically move learners' bodies' introducing muscle memory to feel the correct motion.
- Repeat the details of the skill to instill the thought process of performing the skill. It helps to talk learners through the steps while trying new skills until they are proficient at performing the skill.

Visual references of the support positions are in "The Parent's Guide To: Water Safety And Swim Instruction" and the "Learn to Swim in 8 Lessons or Less' DVD, available winter 2010.

Guided discovery works well with preschool age learners. Instructors ask questions that lead learners to show what they can do at their own pace. Preschool age learners tend to respond better when they feel a sense of control of the pace of their learning. The questions asked are leading questions designed to get learners to try the skills. Simply, put direct instructions in the form of questions. Questions usually begin with "can you" or "can you show me how you." The following are examples of some leading questions:

- Can you show me how you splash the water with your feet?
- Can you show me how you get in the water?
- Can you splash the water with your hands?
- Can you put your elbow in the water?
- Can you put your chin in the water?
- Can you show me how you put your hair in the water?
- Can you put your ear in the water?
- Can you put your other ear in the water?
- Can you take a breath like this and blow slowly?
- Can you take a breath and hold it like this, then blow slowly?
- Can you put your bottom lip in the water and blow slowly?
- Can you take a breath, close your mouth and put both lips in the water then blow slowly?

Feel free to be creative and try other learning styles. As long as the lessons remains safe, fun and focused on the swimming habits and the skills detailed in this book, there is a great chance of achieving success. This program is based on teaching methods and skills arranged in an order that is typically successful with most learners. The intangible that good instructors add is the ability to read each learner and use creativity, skill and quick thinking to adjust and improvise the lesson plans for non-typical learners. Occasionally, it may be necessary to slightly, change the order of the skills. Emphasize the positive aspects of learners' ability. Capitalize on what learners like and do well to help advance to skills that are more difficult.

Within the lesson plans, some skills give an instructor the option to help with support or assistance. "Support" is when the instructor holds the learner or the learner holds something (a wall, floatation device or the instructor) the entire time while practicing a skill. "Assistance" is when the learner begins a skill with support, continues to practice without support and ends with or without support.

Do not leave children alone without adult supervision in or around water, even those who can swim unassisted. An adult should remain close to children at all times. Flotation devices, such as a floaties, life jackets and float suits are not substitutes for close supervision by an adult. Non-swimmers who wear flotation devices need to remain close to an adult. No one, adult or child, should ever swim alone. It is wise for an additional person (young adult or older) to be present and watching whenever an adult is teaching a child or children to swim. That person should be a certified lifeguard or minimally, be able to assist in an emergency by calling 911 or the local emergency phone number and extending a pole, ring buoy, their arm or another object to a person in distress from shore or the side of the pool. That person should avoid distractions by events and activities in, around or away from the pool or body of water were the learning is taking place.

Chapter 2 - Lesson 1

In Lesson 1 learners adjust to the water and the environment, learn good swimming habits and water safety habits. Learners practice breath control skills and learn the importance of the relationship between breath control and relaxing. It is important to focus on breath control first because it is more difficult to swim without the face in the water, although still possible. It is difficult for swimmers to relax if they are not comfortable with the face in the water. Even when swimming on the back, water splashes on the face and often times, the face goes under water when recovering to a vertical position (standing up or treading water).

GOOD HABIT TIP: Always take a breath before putting the face in the water. When coming up for air, release the air under water first. As soon as the mouth and nose clear the surface, take a breath of air immediately and comfortably. Practice and performed this habit always. When this habit is performed as second nature, swimming and learning to swim are comfortable and easy.

Learners also practice gliding and kicking in a prone (horizontal on the front) position. The position of the body and the ability to relax is very important in determining the amount of effort needed to swim well. When swimming in the prone position the face should be in the water and positioned down toward the bottom. The head should be in the water so that waterline is about even with the ears. Holding still with the face down (front float) is typically not as easy for very apprehensive learners and many preschool age learners. Learners who are comfortable and calm in the water may practice the front float before the front glide in Lesson 1. See Lesson 3, page 25 for front float instructions.

GOOD HABIT TIP: When swimming in the prone position, keep the head and face down and the body relaxed. If the head is up, with the face in or out of the water, the body will sink, requiring the swimmer to use more effort to remain horizontal and move in the water. When the head and face are down, the body rises to the surface, making swimming easier.

Even people who can swim benefit from Lesson 1. Learners practice the most basic swimming and water safety skills and habits. Mastering basic swimming and water safety skills and committing them to habit are important to swimming well.

LESSON 1 – 45 MINUTES			
#	TIME ESTIMATE	SKILLS	DESCRIPTION / INSTRUCTIONS
1	2 minutes	Tour the swimming	▪ Walk around the swimming area.

		area.	▪ Notice the entry and exit areas of the facility. ▪ Notice the entry and exit areas of the water. ▪ Notice the shallow and deep-water areas. ▪ Notice the lifeguards and the safety equipment. ▪ Notice the bathrooms.
2	4 minutes	Sit down and review water safety rules.	Discuss the rules and the consequences of not following them. ▪ Never swim alone. ▪ Swim only in supervised and controlled areas. ▪ Children should always ask for permission before entering the water. ▪ Never run around a pool. Walk only. ▪ Do not engage in horseplay, such as dunking and playing too rough. ▪ Do not play on or around the pool ladders. ▪ Never dive in shallow water. ▪ Look for people and objects and be sure the area is clear before jumping or diving in the water. ▪ Do not eat or chew gum while swimming. ▪ Never drink alcohol or take drugs before or during swimming. ▪ Look for and avoid potential hazards. ▪ Get out of the water and leave the area at the first sound of thunder or flash of lightning.
3	1 minute	Flutter kick - sitting on the side of the pool or near shore	▪ Sit on the side of the pool or in water about waist deep or less near the shore. ▪ Hold on to the wall or place your hands on

			the bottom for support. ▪ Extend the legs, point the toes and kick up and down using an alternating leg motion. ▪ Make a little splash by moving the legs slowly. ▪ Keep the knees and ankles loose and floppy. ▪ Then make a big splash by moving the legs faster.
4	2 minutes	Breathing - sitting on the side of the pool or near shore	Prior to putting any part of the face near water, practice breathing techniques while sitting on the side of the pool or on shore. This will prepare learners to practice breath control skills and calm down fearful or apprehensive learners. ▪ Sit on the side of the pool, in water about waist deep or less near the shore or stand in water about waist deep. ▪ Take a breath and exhale slowly through the mouth. Repeat. ▪ Take a breath and exhale slowly through the nose. Repeat. ▪ Take a breath, hold it about three seconds and exhale slowly through the mouth. Repeat. ▪ Take a breath, hold it about three seconds and exhale slowly through the nose. Repeat. ▪ Take a breath, hold it about three seconds and exhale slowly through the mouth and nose. Repeat.
5	1 minute	Get in the water.	Get in the water using the safest method possible. The following are some options: ▪ Using pool stairs—hold on to the railing and walk forward into the water to about

			chest deep. ▪ Using the pool ladder—hold on to the railings and walk backward down the steps into the water to about chest deep. Move away from the ladder and hold the wall or stand in water about chest deep. ▪ Sitting on the side of the pool—roll on to the stomach and let the legs hang down into the water. Slide into water about chest deep. Relax and hold on to the wall. ▪ From the shore—walk forward into the water to about chest deep.
6	1 minute	Get out of the water.	Get out of the water using the safest method possible. The following are some options: ▪ Using pool stairs—turn toward the side of the pool, hold on to the railing and walk forward out of the water. ▪ Using pool ladder—hold on to the railings and walk forward up the steps and out of the water. Move away from the ladder. ▪ At the pool wall—pull the body up and rest elbows on the deck, continue to pull up to the stomach and lie down. Put one knee up on the deck and get out. ▪ Going to shore—face the shore and walk forward out of the water.
7	1 minute	Get in the water, hold the wall or stand in water about waist to shoulder deep and get comfortable.	▪ Holding the wall—bounce up and down past the shoulders to the neck. Do not submerge the head ▪ Standing in water about waist to shoulder deep—walk forward parallel to shore about five feet. Bounce up and down past the shoulders to the neck. Do not submerge the head. Move on an angle toward shore to

			avoid deep water.
8	6 minutes	Holding breaths - blow bubbles with the mouth, nose and then the head in the water	Get in one of the following positions: ▪ Kneel on the second step and put the hands on the top step. ▪ Hold on to the wall with two hands and stand in water about shoulder to neck deep. ▪ Stand in water about shoulder deep and hold the wall with one hand or hold hands with another person (instructor) for support if necessary. ▪ Kneel at the shoreline with the hands on the bottom and the arms in the water about elbow deep. Practice the following steps in order: 1. Take a breath and hold it. Put the chin and bottom lip in the water for about three seconds then blow slowly. Blow bubbles. 2. Take a breath and hold it. Close the mouth and put both lips in the water for about three seconds, then blow slowly. Blow bubbles. 3. Take a breath and hold it. Put the mouth and the tip of the nose in the water for about three seconds, and then blow slowly out of the mouth and nose. Blow bubbles. 4. Take a breath and hold it. Put the mouth and nose in the water for about three seconds, and then blow slowly out of the mouth and nose. Blow bubbles. 5. Take a breath and hold it. Put the face in the water for about three seconds, and then blow slowly out of the mouth and nose. Blow bubbles.

			6. Take a breath and hold it. Put the entire head in the water for about three seconds and then blow slowly out of the mouth and nose. Blow bubbles.
9	4 minutes	Bobbing - with or without support	Every swimming stroke and most aquatic skills require rhythmic breathing. Practice this by bobbing up and down in the water. ▪ Stand in water about chest deep. Extend the arms forward. Keep the arms relaxed. ▪ Take a breath and hold it. ▪ Submerge the mouth, nose, eyes and eventually the entire head for about two seconds. ▪ Exhale underwater slowly (blow bubbles). ▪ Come up and take one breath. Do not shake the head or wipe the face. ▪ Submerge again. ▪ Repeat about four times. Practice bobbing with support by holding on to the wall or by the instructor holding the learner's hands or armpits depending on the size of the learner.
10	4 minutes	Holding breaths - submerge the mouth, nose, face or entire head and pick up toys from beneath the surface	Place objects, such as sinking toys, within reach, on the first and second steps in the pool, about 12 inches deep near shore or hold an object about 12 inches deep underwater. ▪ Take a breath and hold it. ▪ Put at least the mouth in the water but try to put the entire head in the water ▪ Grab the object, blow the bubbles and come up. ▪ Learners should commit to habit; no matter how deep they submerge, exhaling just

			before reaching the surface and taking a breath as soon as the mouth and nose clear the surface. ▪ Try keeping the eyes open. After learners are comfortable submerging with the eyes open, he or she may practice with goggles.
11	4 minutes	Flutter kick - on the front with support	Learners practice with support in any of the following ways: ▪ Holding the wall with two hands and keeping the arms straight. ▪ Placing the hands on the top step and keeping the arms straight. ▪ Placing the hands on the bottom about12 inches from the shoreline and keeping the arms straight. ▪ The instructor faces the learner, lowers the body in the water to a about chest deep and holds his or her sides from underneath near the hips. The learner places the arms on top of the instructor's arms and keeps his or her arms straight. The learner extends the legs straight, close together with the toes pointed. The ankles and knees remain loose as the legs kick up and down. Kick from the hips not the knees. No more than the heels should exit the water. To practice: ▪ Take a breath and hold it. ▪ Put the head down in the water to the ears about three seconds at a time. ▪ Kick continuously. ▪ When a breath is needed, blow bubbles. ▪ Lift the head, take one breath and put the head back in the water. Continue to kick

			when taking a breath. ▪ Repeat the breathing pattern and keep kicking for about 20 to 40 seconds.
12	5 minutes	Front glide - in the streamline position - with or without support and stand up Learners who are comfortable and calm in the water may practice the front float before the front glide. See Lesson 3, page 25 for front float instructions.	Practice the streamline position. ▪ Stand in water about chest deep, on the pool deck or on shore. ▪ Extend the arms straight up. The arms should cover the ears close to the head. ▪ Place one hand on top of the other. ▪ Keep the legs close together and straight. Practice the front glide. ▪ Stand in water about chest deep. ▪ Extend the arms straight up in the streamline position. ▪ Lean forward. ▪ Take a breath and hold it. ▪ Put the face down and head in the water to the ears. ▪ Push off the bottom, glide forward on the surface and keep the legs straight and together with the toes pointed. ▪ Glide about two body lengths. ▪ Blow bubbles. ▪ Bend the knees toward the chest, sweep the hands down and stand up. Practice gliding parallel to the shore. Do not glide toward deep water. To support a learner: ▪ Face the learner and lower the body in the water to about chest deep ▪ Place your hands under the shoulders or hold the learner on the sides near the hips from underneath. ▪ The learner keeps the arms straight on

			top of the instructor's arms or in the streamline position. Practice the front glide pushing off the pool wall. ▪ Hold the wall with one hand and keep the arm straight. ▪ Place the bottom of the feet on the wall with knees bent. ▪ Relax with the shoulders in the water, lean away from the wall and extend the other arm in the direction of travel. ▪ Lean forward. ▪ Take a breath and hold it. ▪ Put the head in the water to the ears. ▪ Let go of the wall and extend the arms in the streamline position. ▪ Push off away from the wall, glide forward and keep the legs straight and together with the toes pointed. ▪ Glide about three body lengths. ▪ Blow bubbles. ▪ Bend the knees toward the chest, sweep the hands down and stand up. If pushing away from the wall or parallel to shore is difficult, try gliding towards the wall, shore or steps.
13	1 minute	Front glide and flutter kick in the streamline position - with or without support	▪ Perform a front glide. ▪ Add a flutter kick. ▪ Kick for a designated distance. ▪ Blow bubbles and stand up. An instructor may provide support as necessary.
14	4 minutes	Front glide and flutter	Hold a kickboard on the sides about four inches

		kick - with a kickboard - with or without support	from the bottom with the thumbs on top. ▪ Extend the arms and keep them straight. ▪ Perform a front glide. ▪ Add the flutter kick. ▪ Go about three body lengths or for about three seconds. ▪ Blow bubbles. ▪ Lift the head and take a breath. Do not push down on the kickboard. ▪ Put the head back in the water and continue. ▪ Repeat and continue as far as possible or to a designated distance. Practice in shallow water. Do not swim toward deep water. An instructor may provide support as necessary.
15	5 minutes	Game	Retrieve sinking toys. Place toys around the area. Practice taking a breath, putting at least the mouth in the water or submerging the entire head. Grab the objects, one at a time. Blow bubbles each time before coming up. Play toypedo catch. A toypedo is a hard rubber sinking toy shaped like a torpedo and distributed by Swimways Corporation. Large toypedoes are about 12 inches long and one and three quarter inches around. Mini toypedoes are about four and one half inches long and three quarters of an inch around. Pass toypedoes underwater only. ▪ Hold the toypedo underwater in front of the body. ▪ Push it in the desired direction and let go. ▪ Watch it glide several feet away.

			Practice passing the toypedo with at least the mouth in the water. When possible, pass and catch the toypedo with the head completely underwater and the eyes open. ▪ Take a breath. ▪ Submerge the mouth, nose eyes or entire head. ▪ Pass or catch the toypedo. ▪ Blow bubbles and come up. ("Blow when you throw" or "blow when you catch")

It may take fearful and less coordinated learners up to about five lessons to master breath control. Be patient and persistent. After mastering breath control, learning other swimming skills are easier.

GOOD HABIT TIP: Breathing water in the nose is an uncomfortable feeling. This may cause a setback for fearful learners. Do not worry; this also happens to good swimmers. Reassure the learner that this is part of the learning process and remind him or her to breathe air not water.

GOOD HABBIT TIP: Try to practice flutter kicking with the head down. The purpose of this drill is to continue focusing on breath control, relaxing and body position as well as kicking. Do not force the issue. If putting the face down and head in the water is uncomfortable for learners, practice breathing and blowing bubbles with the mouth or mouth and nose while kicking until learners are comfortable putting the entire head down.

PRACTICE TIP: Fearful learners make some common mistakes, such as holding their breath after reaching the surface and then exhaling, forgetting to inhale after reaching the surface, inhaling before reaching the surface and exhaling intermittently underwater. To emphasize exhaling slowly underwater and then inhaling after reaching the surface, have a bubble-blowing contest. Take a breath, put the mouth in the water and blow bubbles slowly as long as possible. Then take a breath and repeat a few more times.

PRACTICE TIP: Some people have trouble stretching out in a prone position because they may feel a lack of control by not being able to touch the bottom with their feet. Continue to practice with support and gradually remove the support.

PRACTICE TIP: You may substitute practicing with a kickboard by holding a foam noodle in the hands and extending the arms forward.

PRACTICE TIP: Preschool learners may not be comfortable practicing with a kickboard on the front and/or the back. Do not force anyone to practice with a kickboard. Continue to provide support or assistance until learners are comfortable swimming with assistance or no support at all.

Chapter 3 - Lesson 2

In Lesson 2 learners continue to practice the skills practiced and learned in Lesson 1. Supine (horizontal on the back) position skills are introduced and practiced. Although floating and swimming on the back are uncomfortable for some learners initially, it is important to practice and master these skills. Floating and swimming on the back are also important survival skills. If a swimmer it too tired to swim, too ill or too injured, recovering on the back is easier. Breathing is easier when the body is relaxed and the face out of the water.

GOOD HABIT TIP: When swimming on the back, maintain good body position by keeping the head back, ears in the water, looking straight up, arching the back so that the stomach rises up to the surface and relaxing. The feet should remain slightly below the surface.

GOOD HABIT TIP: When flutter kicking on the back, kick up until the leg completely extends slightly under the surface. No more than the big toe should come out of the water. On the downbeat, keep the leg straight and start moving the leg downward. Complete the downbeat by bending the knee slightly. Start the upbeat by kicking upward until the leg completely extends again. Kick vigorous enough to keep the chest and stomach on the surface using an alternating kicking motion.

GOOD HABIT TIP: When pushing away from the wall in the supine position, water may wash over the face, especially when pushing hard. Remember to blow out of the nose to prevent water from going in the nose.

LESSON 2 – 37 MINUTES 30 SECONDS			
#	TIME ESTIMATE	SKILLS	DESCRIPTION / INSTRUCTIONS
1	1 minute	Flutter kick - sitting on the side of the pool or near shore	See Lesson 1, page 6.
2	1 minute	Breathing - sitting on the side of the pool or near shore	See Lesson 1, page 7.
3	30 seconds	Get in the water.	See Lesson 1, page 7.
4	4 minutes	Holding breaths - blow bubbles with the mouth, nose and then	See Lesson 1, page 9.

		the head in the water	
5	4 minutes	Bobbing - with or without support	See Lesson 1, page 10.
6	3 minutes	Front glide and flutter kick - with or without support	See Lesson 1, page 13.
7	3 minutes	Front glide and flutter kick - with a kickboard - with or without support	See Lesson 1, page 13.
8	5 minutes	Back float - with or without support and stand up	Stand in water about waist to chest deep, on the deck or shore. Practice the back float position. ▪ Extend the arms over the head slightly wider than shoulder width apart. Relax the arms and bend the elbows, slightly. ▪ Hold the head back. ▪ Arch the back. Practice the back float in water about chest deep. The key to floating on the back and front is to relax. ▪ Submerge in the water to about shoulder depth and lean back. ▪ Put the head back with the ears in the water. Look straight up. ▪ Arch the back and lift the feet off the ground. Kick until chest and stomach rise to the surface. ▪ Extend the arms over the head and slightly wider than shoulder width apart. Relax the arms and bend the elbows, slightly. Position the hands slightly under the water, about one inch with the palms

			facing up. To stand up: ▪ Take a breath and hold it. ▪ Lift the head, lean forward and bend at the waist. ▪ Turn the palms down, sweep the arms downward, and out then in and out as needed for balance. ▪ Drop the feet to the bottom and stand up. To support a learner: ▪ Stand behind the learner and submerge in the water to shoulder depth. Make sure to submerge deep enough to allow the learner's head to be in the water while resting on the instructor's shoulder. ▪ Instruct the learner to put the ears in the water and look straight up. ▪ Position the hands underneath the learner's legs, hips or small of the back depending on the learner's size and comfort level. The learner is relaxed when the body is loose, the head is back with ears in the water, the legs are not stiff and the feet are slightly under the water. When the learner begins to relax— ▪ Position the hands on the learner's back below the shoulder blades. ▪ Extend the arms and move the learner's head off the shoulders. As the learner becomes more comfortable, move

			backwards a few steps. Gliding some helps the learner's buoyancy. Change the position of the hands. ▪ Position one hand on the learner's back in the middle and the other hand under the head. ▪ Extend the arms so that the learner's head is away from your body. ▪ When more relaxed, remove the hand from under the learner's back. ▪ When more relaxed, remove the hand from under the learner's head and back. ▪ Support the learner to help him or her stand up.
9	5 minutes	Back glide – with the arms at the side then stand up	Practice the back glide. ▪ Stand in water about chest deep. ▪ Face the opposite direction of the intended direction of travel. Swim parallel to the deep area. Do not swim towards the deep area. ▪ Submerge to in the water to shoulder depth and lean back. Extend the arms straight out to the sides. ▪ Put the head back with ears in the water. Look straight up. ▪ Arch the back, push off the bottom, and glide back. ▪ Sweep the arms to the hips to add momentum. Keep the arms straight, relaxed and slightly underwater. ▪ Glide until the momentum slows and stand up. Practice the back glide pushing off the pool wall.

			Begin in the starting position for supine position strokes. ▪ Face the wall and hold on with two hands. Place the balls of both feet against the wall with the knees bent. Position the knees between the arms. ▪ Relax and lean back. ▪ Put the head back with the ears in the water. Perform the back glide. ▪ Gently push away from the wall. Exhale through the nose to keep water out. ▪ Arch the back so the chest, stomach and legs rise to the surface. ▪ Keep the legs straight and together with the toes pointed. ▪ Keep the arms by the sides. ▪ Glide until the momentum slows and stand up.
10	3 minutes	Back glide and flutter kick - with or without support	▪ Perform a back glide. ▪ Add a flutter kick. ▪ Continue to a designated distance and stand up. An instructor may provide support as necessary. ▪ Place one hand under the back and one hand under the head or just one hand under the head. ▪ Extend the arms and move back as the learner pushes off away from the wall.
11	3 minutes	Back glide and flutter kick - with kickboard - with or without	Begin in the starting position in water about chest deep or hold the pool wall. When starting by pushing away from the pool wall, hold the

		support	kickboard with the thumbs and index fingers. Hold the wall with the other fingers. If this is too difficult, hold the kickboard with one hand and hold the wall with the other hand. ▪ Start with a back glide. ▪ Hold a kickboard on the sides and in the middle of the kickboard with fingers on top. Do not wrap the arms around the kickboard (hugging the kickboard). ▪ Squeeze the kickboard against the chest. ▪ Perform a back glide. ▪ Add the flutter kick. ▪ Continue to a designated distance and stand up. An instructor may provide support as necessary.
12	5 minutes	Game	Retrieve sinking toys and play toypedo catch. See Lesson 1, page 14.

PRACTICE TIP: When stopping the swimming motion in the supine position, especially in a pool near the wall, roll over on the front and grab the wall or stand up. By doing this, you are practicing a rolling motion in the horizontal position from the back to the front. You are practicing the first step of an open turn for supine position strokes. An open turn on the back is the way a swimmer changes directions and continues swimming in the opposite direction. You are also practicing the body roll motion, which is necessary for swimming the front and back crawl and breathing when swimming the front crawl. Practice this skill by doing the following:

- *Let go of the kickboard if you are using one.*
- *Take a breath and hold it.*
- *Roll over on the front with the face down.*
- *Glide forward and blow bubbles.*
- *Grab the wall and pull up or stand up.*

PRACTICE TIP: You may substitute using a kickboard by holding a foam noodle across the chest and under the arms.

PRACTICE TIP: Learners having trouble relaxing on the back and are supported by an instructor should rest the hands on the stomach until he or she can relax the arms by the side.

PRACTICE TIP: Instructors may want to use this alternate method to introduce the back float to learners. The learner holds the pool wall, positions the head back with the ears in the water and presses the belly button against the wall. Then the learner lets go of the wall. The instructor stands behind the learner and provides support or assistance as the learner leans back and moves to the back float position.

Chapter 4 - Lesson 3

In Lesson 3 learners continue to practice the skills practiced and learned in Lessons 1 and 2. Front float and propulsion skills on the back and front (finning and front crawl) are introduced and practiced. Learners practice jumping in the water from the sitting position (little jumps), leveling off and swimming to safety.

The front float emphasizes the most efficient prone position, the primary skill used when survival floating and relaxing on the front with the face in the water.

PRACTICE TIP: Some people have trouble stretching out in a prone position and floating in a still and relaxed manner. Continue to practice with support, either holding the wall, putting hands on the top step, putting the hands on the bottom near the shoreline or with an instructor's support. Gradually remove the support as learners' comfort level increases.

The front crawl is commonly considered the fastest stroke in swimming which is why competitive swimmers use this stroke in freestyle races. Often times people refer to the front crawl as "freestyle". When learning the front crawl, some learners may not bring their arms out of the water completely after completing the underwater pull and returning the arm to the forward extended position (the recovery). The primary focus should be on the underwater pull until comfort and coordination are achieved. Use an alternating pattern.

GOOD HABIT TIP: Begin with the arms extended forward. Relax the arms and hands, sweep down, and pull back. Pull all the way back to the hips and legs. Try to use long strokes and not short "doggie paddle" strokes.

Occasionally, preschool age learners may not be coordinated enough to move the arms or legs using an alternating pattern. It may be naturally more comfortable to use simultaneous (breaststroke) arm and/or leg movements. This should not be discouraged. Instead, emphasize the motion. The goal is for learners to propel the body. Continue to focus on breath control, relaxing and body position. As coordination improves, specific swimming strokes can be emphasized and learned.

Swimmers who are more comfortable on the back should practice leveling off on the back first. See Lesson 4, page 35 for leveling off on the back. When practicing jumping into the water, some learners, especially preschool age learners, may require assistance to come up to the surface, initially. This is very common, so provide assistance as necessary.

LESSON 3 – 39 MINUTES 15 SECONDS			
#	TIME ESTIMATE	SKILLS	DESCRIPTION / INSTRUCTIONS
1	15 seconds	Get in the water.	See Lesson 1, page 7.
2	2 minutes	Bobbing	See Lesson 1, page 10.
3	1 minutes	Holding breaths – underwater	▪ Stand in water about chest deep. Hold the wall or the instructor's hands for support if necessary. ▪ Take a breath and hold it. ▪ Submerge the head for about five seconds. ▪ Blow bubbles and come up. ▪ Practice two more times.
4	3 minutes	Front glide and flutter kick - with a kickboard - with or without support	See Lesson 1, page 13.
5	5 minutes	Front float	Standing in water about chest deep— ▪ Extend the arms forward a bit wider than shoulder width apart. ▪ Relax and lean forward. ▪ Take a breath and hold it. ▪ Put the head down in the water to the ears. ▪ Lift the legs off the bottom. ▪ Keep the legs extended straight and relaxed. ▪ Be still, relax and float in the prone position for about five seconds. ▪ Blow bubbles. ▪ Bend the knees toward the chest, sweep the hands down and stand up. Practice the front float with support in any of the following ways: ▪ Hold the wall with two hands keeping the

			arms straight at about shoulder width apart. ▪ Place the hands on the top step keeping the arms straight. ▪ Place the hands on the bottom about12 inches from the shoreline keeping the arms straight. Support a learner in any of the following ways: ▪ Hold the learner under the shoulders. ▪ Hold the learner's wrist from underneath. ▪ Hold the learner near the hips from underneath. The learner keeps the arms straight on top of the instructor's arms. When the learner puts the head in the water, pull the learner forward about one body length to generate enough momentum to help the legs rise to the surface. Remove the support for a couple seconds if possible.
6	2 minutes	Back float	See Lesson 2, page 18.
7	3 minutes	Back glide and flutter kick - with a kickboard - with or without support	See Lesson 2, page 21.
8	4 minutes	Flutter kick on the back - with finning	Practice the finning motion standing in water about chest deep. ▪ Relax and let the arms hang straight past the hips with the hands turned in, palms facing the legs. ▪ Move the arms away from the body about 12 inches and push the water back toward the legs. ▪ Repeat this motion continuously and

			quickly. Practice flutter kicking on the back and finning. ▪ Start with a back glide. ▪ Add the flutter kick. ▪ Add finning. ▪ Maintain supine body position while swimming. ▪ Swim to a desired distance in shallow water and stand up or roll over on the front, blow bubbles and stand up.
9	6 minutes	Front crawl	Stand in water about chest deep, lean forward and practice the front crawl alternating arm motion. ▪ Extend the arms forward. ▪ Relax the hands with the palms facing down, the fingers straight and almost touching each other. Do not hold the fingers tightly together. Do not spread the fingers wide apart. Do not hold the hands in a cupped position. ▪ Bend the elbow of one arm slightly and sweep the arm down. ▪ Keep the arm close to the body and push the water back past the hip. ▪ Start the recovery by bending the elbow up and swinging the arm out to the side. ▪ Keep the palm facing back and continue moving the arm to the forward extended position. ▪ Place the hand in the water in line with the shoulder with the elbow slightly bent and the fingertips down. ▪ Extend the arm forward, slightly under

			the surface and repeat the motion. ▪ Alternate the arms using this movement. ▪ Start the pull of the extended arm while the other arm is just past the middle of the middle of the recovery. Practice the front crawl in the prone position. ▪ Start with a front glide. ▪ Add the flutter kick. ▪ Begin moving the arms. ▪ Keep the head down and straight. Do not swing the head from side to side. ▪ Move the arms about five strokes blow bubbles and stand up. Depending on the size of the learner and the instructor, helping learners move the arms for the purpose of feeling the mechanics of the stroke can be accomplished in the following ways: ▪ The instructor stands behind the learner on land or in the water. - or - ▪ The learner sits or stands on the instructor's thigh just above the knee. ▪ The instructor holds the learner's wrist from underneath with his or her thumbs pointing up and the fingers placed on top of the learner's hand. ▪ The instructor moves the learner's arms properly. Reach forward, sweep down and pull the water back. Bend the elbow up and swing the arm to the outside. Then reach forward and pull again. Practice moving one arm at a time. Then move the arms using a continuous

			alternating pattern. - or - ▪ The instructor stands next to the learner facing the same direction. ▪ The learner does a front float, relaxes and allows the instructor to move the arms. ▪ While the learner is doing a front float, the instructor reaches over the learner and holds the learner's wrist from underneath with his or her thumbs pointing up and the fingers placed on top of the learner's hand. ▪ If necessary, support the learner in a horizontal position by placing a knee under the learner's body. ▪ Move the learner's arms properly. ▪ The learner blows bubbles and stands up.
10	5 minutes	Level off on the front and swim to safety (a place to hold on or stand up, such as a wall or shallow water).	Practice leveling off on the front. ▪ Stand in water about shoulder to neck deep. Face the wall or shore. ▪ Take a breath. ▪ Extend the arms, lean forward, put the face and head down in the water. ▪ Kick to help the body rise to the surface. ▪ Continue kicking and pull with the arms to safety. Practice submerging and leveling off. ▪ Stand in water about shoulder to neck deep. Face the wall or shore. ▪ Take a breath. ▪ Bend the knees and submerge the entire head. ▪ Sweep the arms down and/or push off the

			bottom with the feet. ▪ Blow bubbles and come up. ▪ Take another breath. ▪ Level off and swim to safety.
11	3 minutes	Little jump - level off on the front and swim to the wall	If you are in a pool practice little jumps. ▪ Sit on the side of the pool. Place the hands on the edge and the feet against the wall. ▪ Take a breath. ▪ Push away from the wall and enter the water. ▪ Let the body submerge. ▪ Sweep the arms down and/or push off the bottom with the feet. ▪ Blow bubbles while coming up. ▪ After reaching the surface, take a breath, turn around and face the wall. ▪ Level off and swim back to the wall.
12	5 minutes	Game	Play toypedo catch and dive for sinking toys.

GOOD HABIT TIP: When practicing breath holding, do not hyperventilate before taking a breath. Relax, take a breath and hold it. Do not have breath-holding contest. Repeated extended breath holding can also be dangerous. These bad habits may cause a swimmer to blackout while underwater.

Chapter 5 - Lesson 4

In Lesson 4 learners continue to practice the skills practiced and learned in Lessons 1, 2 and 3. Bobbing to safety, front crawl with breathing, front crawl and rolling on to the back and floating, and leveling off on the back are introduced and practiced.

In addition to practicing rhythmic breathing, bobbing to safety is a safety skill that teaches learners to get to safety without swimming in a horizontal position. Bobbing is an important safety skill because if a swimmer is too tired to swim, too injured or too ill and it prevents conventional swimming, bobbing to safety is an option.

PRACTICE TIP: Begin by practicing bobbing in shallow water. As learners' confidence and skills improve, gradually move to deeper water. Practice bobbing away from the wall or shore and back to safety. Submerge in water over the head, push off the bottom or use a breaststroke kick (see Lesson 5, page 38) and the simultaneous down, out and back sweeping motion of the hands to reach the surface.

Swimming on the front then rolling on to the back and floating is another important safety skill. If a swimmer becomes exhausted, ill or injured he or she can roll over on the back to rest and recover. In addition, this skill is the first step to learning rotary breathing (see Lesson 6 and 7, page 42 and 46). This skill allows learners to practice rolling the body without lifting the head.

GOOD HABIT TIP: When rolling over from front to back, blow bubbles first, roll over and do not lift the head. As the face exits the water, put the head back, ears in the water and kick some to help keep the body horizontal. After taking a breath, it may be necessary to blow through the nose to prevent splashing water from entering the nose.

Leveling off on the back is just as effective and easier for some people, as leveling off on the front. The objective is to move the body to a horizontal position and swim.

LESSON 4 – 40 MINUTES 15 SECONDS			
#	TIME ESTIMATE	SKILLS	DESCRIPTION / INSTRUCTIONS
1	15 seconds	Get in the water.	See Lesson 1, page 7.
2	1 minute	Bobbing	See Lesson 1, page 10.
3	4 minutes	Bobbing - away from the wall or shore and	Practice bobbing away from the wall or shore and back to safety.

		back to safety	▪ Stand in water about chest deep. ▪ Bend the knees to lower the body to shoulder depth. Relax the legs and body. ▪ Extend the arms forward and slightly wider than shoulder width. Relax the arms and position the arms and hands on the surface. Turn the palms down. ▪ Take a breath and submerge until the head is completely underwater. ▪ After one or two seconds, blow bubbles. ▪ Sweep the hands down, lean forward and push off the bottom forward and up. ▪ When the mouth and nose clear the surface, calmly, take another breath. Do not shake the head or wipe face. ▪ Repeat without stopping until the water is about neck deep. ▪ Turn around and bob to safety.
4	1 minute	Holding breaths – underwater	See Lesson 3, page 25.
5	1 minute	Front float	See Lesson 3, page 25.
6	3 minutes	Front glide and flutter kick - with a kickboard - with or without support	See Lesson 1, page 13.
7	1 minute	Back float	See Lesson 2, page 18.
8	3 minutes	Back glide and flutter kick - with a kickboard - with or without support	See Lesson 2, page 21.
9	5 minutes	Front crawl – with breathing - with or without assistance	Practice the front crawl and add rhythmic breathing to swim a longer distance. Ultimately, rotary breathing (rolling the body and turning the head to the side to take a breath) is best. Until

			Lesson 6 or 7, learners may lift the head to breathe. ▪ Start with a front glide and flutter kick. ▪ Take about four strokes. ▪ Blow bubbles. ▪ Lift the head and take a breath. ▪ Put the head down in the water and continue swimming. ▪ Repeat to a designated distance. Provide assistance to help the learner breathe. ▪ Stand about four feet in front of the learner. ▪ The learner swims toward the instructor. ▪ After about three strokes, remind the learner to blow bubbles. ▪ Place your hands under the learner's chest or shoulders; lift the learner allowing him or her to breathe. ▪ After the learner takes a breath, lower the learner into the water to continue swimming. ▪ Repeat to a designated distance. As learners gain strength and confidence, assistance will no longer be necessary. To decrease assistance: ▪ Help the learner breathe every other breath. Be sure to tell the learner which breath he or she will take without assistance. ▪ Be ready to lift learners who cannot come up for air. When learners exhale underwater, the next instinct is to inhale. Do not let the learner inhale water.

10	5 minutes	Front crawl roll over and back float	Practice the front crawl roll over and back float. ▪ Start with a front glide and flutter kick. ▪ Take about four strokes. The last should sweep down and across the body instead of straight back to begin the roll on to the back. ▪ Blow bubbles. ▪ Roll over on the back. Keep the head in the water. ▪ Lean back and kick some to keep the body horizontal on the surface. ▪ Relax and rest in the supine position for about four seconds. ▪ Stand up. To continue swimming to a designated distance: ▪ Do not stand up, but continue from the back float. ▪ Take a breath. ▪ Reach over the body and forward and roll over on to the front. Keep the head down, face in the water. ▪ Continue swimming the front crawl. ▪ Repeat to a designated distance. To provide assistance: ▪ The learner swims toward the instructor. ▪ After about four strokes, remind the learner to blow bubbles and roll over. ▪ Place one hand under the learners shoulder and the other hand on top of the other shoulder. ▪ Push up with the hand from underneath. ▪ Gently push down with the hand on top and guide the learner on to the back.

			▪ Slide the hand that was on top under the head and the other hand under the back.
11	3 minutes	Flutter kick on the back - with finning	See Lesson 3, page 26.
12	5 minutes	Level off on the back and swim to safety.	Practice leveling off on the back. ▪ Stand in water about shoulder to neck deep. Turn away from the wall or shore. ▪ Lean back and put the head in the water to the ears. Look up. ▪ Kick to help the body rise to the surface. ▪ Continue kicking and finning. ▪ Swim to safety. Practice submerging and leveling off. ▪ Stand in water about shoulder to neck deep. Turn away from the wall or shore. ▪ Take a breath. ▪ Bend the knees and submerge the entire head. ▪ Sweep the arms down and/or push off the bottom with the feet. ▪ Blow bubbles and come up. ▪ Take another breath. ▪ Level off on the back and swim to safety.
13	3 minutes	Little jump - level off on the back and swim to the wall	If you are in a pool practice little jumps, leveling off on the back and swimming to safety. ▪ Sit on the side of the pool. ▪ Jump in the water. ▪ After reaching the surface, take a breath and lean back toward the wall. ▪ Level off and swim back to the wall.
14	5 minutes	Game	Play toypedo catch. Play noodle leap frog.

			▪ Place a foam noodle under the armpits, relax and rest on the noodle. ▪ The instructor positions another noodle about five feet in front of the learner and holds it to keep it from floating away. ▪ Remove the noodle from the armpits with the hands. ▪ Take a breath. ▪ Throw the noodle over the head and behind. The body will submerge. ▪ Come up and take a breath. ▪ Put the head down in the water and level off on the front. ▪ Swim the front crawl to the next noodle and rest on the noodle. ▪ The instructor places the discarded noodle in front of the learner. ▪ Repeat to a designated distance.

Chapter 6 – Lesson 5

In Lesson 5 learners continue to practice the skills practiced and learned in Lessons 1, 2, 3 and 4. Big jumps (jumping in the water from a standing position) and breaststroke kick are introduced and practiced. Learners coordinate a powerful simultaneous leg motion allowing the body to move a longer distance with less effort. The breaststroke kick is used with two resting strokes, elementary backstroke and breaststroke. In addition the breaststroke kick is one of three kicks used to tread water (remaining in one area in a vertical position, with the head above the water). When swimming elementary backstroke and breaststroke, swimmers kick with power and glide. During the glide, swimmers can rest and recover.

LESSON 5 – 37 MINUTES 15 SECONDS			
#	TIME ESTIMATE	SKILLS	DESCRIPTION / INSTRUCTIONS
1	15 seconds	Get in the water.	See Lesson 1, page 7.
2	3 minutes	Front glide and flutter kick - with a kickboard - with or without assistance	See Lesson 1, page 13.
3	3minutes	Back glide and flutter kick - with a kickboard - with or without assistance	See Lesson 2, page 21.
4	3 minutes	Front crawl – with breathing - with or without assistance	See Lesson 3, page 32.
5	3 minutes	Flutter kick on the back -with finning	See Lesson 3, page 26.
6	4 minutes	Front crawl rollover and back float	See Lesson 4, page 34.
7	5 minutes	Big jump - swim back to the wall on front and back	Practice big jumps into the water from a standing position and swim back to the wall on the front and back. Jump into water deeper than the swimmer's height. ▪ Stand at the edge of the pool and curl the

			toes over the edge. ▪ Jump out away from the wall. ▪ Return to the surface. ▪ Level of on the front or back and swim to the wall.
8	3 minutes	Breaststroke kick - sitting on the side of the pool or near shore	Sit on the side of the pool or in water about waist deep near shore and practice the breaststroke kick. ▪ Place the hands on the edge of the pool or slightly behind the body on the bottom of the lake, ocean, river or creek for support. ▪ Extend the legs and point the toes. ▪ Flex the ankles, bend the knees and move them slightly UP toward the chest. ▪ Drop the heels down and move the legs OUT (apart and wide). ▪ Continue moving the legs out in a circular motion out, squeeze them back TOGETHER straight then point the toes. ▪ Hold the legs in the straight position for about three seconds and repeat. The power phase of the kick is the motion of the legs squeezing together to the straight position. Then the body glides for a few seconds before the kicking motion repeats.
9	4 minutes	Breaststroke kick on the back - with a kickboard - with or without assistance	Practice swimming on the back using the breaststroke kick. Use a kickboard and add this drill to the practice routine. ▪ Begin in the starting position for supine position skills. Hold the kickboard. ▪ Push off and glide on the back. ▪ Flex the ankles and bend the knees slightly UP. ▪ Drop the heels down and move the legs

			OUT (apart and wide). ▪ Continue moving the legs in a circular motion out and squeeze them TOGETHER straight. ▪ Point the toes and GLIDE. An instructor may provide necessary assistance or support; see Lesson 2, page 21.
10	4 minutes	Breaststroke kick - on the front - with a kickboard - with or without assistance	Practice swimming on the front using the breaststroke kick. Use a kickboard and add this drill to the practice routine. ▪ Begin in the starting position for prone position skills. Hold the kickboard. ▪ Take a breath and put the face down and head in the water. ▪ Hold the kickboard with both hands, push off, and glide on the front. ▪ Flex the ankles and bend the knees slightly UP toward the chest. ▪ Move the heels toward the surface, but not above the surface and move the legs OUT (apart and wide). ▪ Continue moving the legs in a circular motion out and squeeze them TOGETHER straight. ▪ Point the toes and GLIDE. ▪ Blow bubbles. ▪ Lift the head and breathe. ▪ Put the head back down in the water and repeat. Think the rhythm; blow bubbles, breathe, head back down, kick and glide, blow bubbles, breathe, head back down, kick and glide. An instructor may provide assistance as necessary.

11	5 minutes	Game	Play jump games. Always curl the toes over the edge. ▪ Jump in the water, level off and swim to a designated distance. ▪ Jump in the water, level off and swim to a foam noodle and rest. ▪ Jump in the water, level off and swim back to the wall. ▪ Jump out as far away from the wall as possible and into the water. Swim to a designated distance or back to the wall.

GOOD HABIT TIPS: Avoid the common mistakes when practicing the breaststroke kick. Do not exert power kicking out and wide. Exert power when squeezing the legs together. When starting the kick, bend just slightly at the waist. Bending too much or not at all will not allow swimmers to maximize the power of the kick. Extend the body at the end of the kick motion. Do not break the surface with the feet. Keep the feet slightly underwater. Keep the ankles flexed during the kick motion. Point the toes during the glide.

Chapter 7 – Lesson 6

In Lesson 6 learners continue to practice the skills practiced and learned in Lessons 1, 2, 3, 4 and 5. The initial steps to rotary breathing and survival floating are introduced and practiced. Rolling the body, while maintaining a horizontal position is necessary for breathing to the side when swimming the front crawl. Learners will practice rolling the body from the front to back and from the back to front to prepare to learn rotary breathing. This drill also emphasizes breath control, relaxing and body position. Survival floating is a way to remain buoyant in deep water for several minutes or even hours with little effort.

LESSON 6 – 40 MINUTES			
#	TIME ESTIMATE	SKILLS	DESCRIPTION / INSTRUCTIONS
1	1 minutes	Jump in and swim back to the wall.	See Lessons 4 and 5, pages 35 and 37.
2	3 minutes	Front glide and flutter kick - with a kickboard - with or without assistance	See Lesson 1, page 13.
3	3 minutes	Back glide and flutter kick - with a kickboard - with or without assistance	See Lesson 2, page 21.
4	3 minutes	Back glide and breaststroke kick - with a kickboard - with or without assistance	See Lesson 5, page 38.
5	3 minutes	Front glide and breaststroke kick - with a kickboard - with or without assistance	See Lesson 5, page 39.
6	3 minutes	Front crawl - with breathing - with or without assistance	See Lesson 4, page 32.
7	3 minutes	Flutter kick on the back -with finning	See Lesson 3, page 26.

8	5 minutes	Front float rollover and back float then rollover and front float	The purpose of this drill is to practice rolling the body without lifting the head out of the water. By doing so, learning rotary breathing will be easier. ▪ Start with a front float for about five seconds. ▪ Blow bubbles. ▪ Sweep down and across the body with one hand. ▪ Roll over on to the back and float for about five seconds. Do not lift the head. Keep the head back with the ears in the water. ▪ Kick some to help the body move up and remain horizontal on the surface. ▪ Relax and breathe normal. ▪ Exhale through the nose to keep splashing water out. ▪ Take a breath and roll over on the front. Do not lift the head up or lean forward. Roll the face down in the water. ▪ Relax in the front float position. ▪ Repeat about four times. To assist a learner, follow the same method described in Lesson 4 on page 33 (front crawl roll over and back float).
9	5 minutes	Front crawl - rollover on the back and take <u>one</u> breath, then continue swimming on the front	Swimming the front crawl, rolling on to the back, taking one breath, rolling back on the front and continuing to swim on the front is the second step to learning rotary breathing. To practice this skill: ▪ Take about four strokes, blow bubbles and roll on to the back. ▪ Take <u>one</u> breath. ▪ Reach across the body and forward, roll

			back on to the front and continue swimming. Roll back to the front the in the direction rolled from. Do not "log" roll over and over. ▪ Repeat after about every four strokes.
10	2 minutes	Front crawl - roll on to the side and take <u>one</u> breath, then continue swimming on the front	When learners are proficient at swimming the front crawl, rolling on to the back and taking <u>one</u> breath, try moving on to the final step of learning rotary breathing with the front crawl. ▪ After about four strokes, blow bubbles and roll as if rolling on to the back. Roll only half way (on the side) and turn the head until the mouth clear the surface. ▪ Take <u>one</u> breath. ▪ Continue the arm stroke. ▪ Put the face back in the water. Repeat after about two or four strokes.
11	1 minutes	Jellyfish Float	The jellyfish float is similar to a front float. The difference is the head, arms and legs hang down, like a jellyfish.
12	3 minutes	Survival Float	Practice survival floating. ▪ Start by doing a front float. ▪ Remain face down with the hands floating on the surface for about five seconds. ▪ The legs hang, similar to the jellyfish float. ▪ Blow bubbles. Sweep the hands down and kick a little to help raise the head. Lift the head up. ▪ Take a breath. ▪ Put the head down and float again. ▪ Repeat.

13	5 minutes	Game	Play deep-water toypedo catch. Playing deep-water toypedo catch is a fun way to practice survival floating. However, it may not be practical to play this game if you are swimming in open water, such as a lake. The visibility may be difficult if not impossible to see more than a few feet. If the toypedo is dropped, it could be lost forever. The object is to relax, play catch in deep water and avoid letting the toypedo to sink to the bottom. Use goggles to see the toypedo better. ▪ Take a breath. ▪ Put the head in the water and float. ▪ Pass the toypedo to the other person. ▪ Blow bubbles. ▪ Lift the head and take a breath. ▪ Put the head back in the water and float. ▪ Catch the toypedo. ▪ Blow bubbles. ▪ Lift the head and take a breath. ▪ Put the head back in the water and float. ▪ Pass the toypedo again. ▪ Repeat. Play on a boogie board or surfboard. In open water, practice paddling and riding a boogie board or surfboard.

Chapter 8 – Lesson 7

In Lesson 7 learners continue to practice the skills practiced and learned in Lessons 1, 2, 3, 4, 5 and 6. Front crawl with rotary breathing, elementary backstroke and treading water are introduced and practiced. When rotary breathing is used, the front crawl is a smooth and efficient swimming stroke.

Two survival skills, treading water and elementary backstroke, help people maintain buoyancy or swim with little effort. Treading water requires more effort than survival floating because the head remains above the surface. Elementary backstroke is a good stroke to swim when swimmers need to survive, rest and recover because of exhaustion, injury or illness.

For example, a swimmer working out in open water becomes exhausted and is hyperventilating about one half mile from shore. To survive, the swimmer rolls over on to the back and swims elementary backstroke while recovering. When the swimmer recovers, he resumes the workout.

LESSON 7 – 40 MINUTES 15 SECONDS			
#	TIME ESTIMATE	SKILLS	DESCRIPTION / INSTRUCTIONS
1	15 seconds	Jump in and swim back to the wall.	See Lessons 4 and 5, pages 35 and 37.
2	3 minutes	Front glide and flutter kick - with a kickboard - with or without assistance	See Lesson 1, page 13.
3	3 minutes	Back glide and flutter kick - with a kickboard - with or without assistance	See Lesson 2, page 21.
4	3 minutes	Back glide and breaststroke kick - with a kickboard - with or without assistance	See Lesson 5, page 38.
5	3 minutes	Front glide and breaststroke kick - with a kickboard - with or without assistance	See Lesson 5, page 39.

6	3 minutes	Front crawl - with breathing - with assistance	See Lesson 4, page 32.
7	3 minutes	Flutter kick on the back - with finning	See Lesson 3, page 26.
8	2 minutes	Front crawl - rollover on the back and take <u>one</u> breath, then continue swimming on the front	See Lesson 6, page 42.
9	6 minutes	Front crawl - with rotary breathing	Practice the rotary breathing head turn. ▪ Stand in water about chest deep or kneel in water about waist deep. ▪ Extend the arms forward. Place the hand opposite of the turning direction on the wall, top step or the bottom near shore for support. Keep the arm near the surface. ▪ Relax the arm on the side of the turning direction so it is not on the surface. ▪ Put the head down in the water. ▪ Blow bubbles. ▪ Turn the head and roll the body until the mouth and nose exit the water. Keep the side of the head in the water. ▪ Take a breath and put the face back down in the water for about three seconds. ▪ Repeat about five times. When learners are proficient at swimming front, crawl, rolling on to the back and taking <u>one</u> breath, move on to the final step and swim the front crawl using rotary breathing. ▪ After about four strokes, blow bubbles and roll as if rolling on to the back. Roll

			only half way (on the side) and turn the head until the mouth and nose clear the surface. Keep the side of the head in the water. ▪ Take one breath. ▪ Continue the arm stroke. ▪ Put the face back in the water ▪ Repeat after about two or four strokes. The timing of the arm stroke with the breathing is important to maintain an efficient stroke. ▪ While the arm of the non-breathing side is pulling, blow bubbles. ▪ Begin the pull of the extended arm on the breathing side. ▪ Roll the body and turn the head. Finish the pull of the arm on the breathing side. ▪ Take a breath. The hand on the breathing side should be out of the water with the elbow high and starting to move forward to the extended position. ▪ Put the face back down in the water. ▪ Put the hand on the breathing side in the water and start another pull. At this point the arm on the non-breathing side should be about half of the way through the pull. ▪ Blow bubbles slowly after the face returns to the water. Think the rhythm; pull and breathe head back down, blow bubbles.
10	4 minutes	Elementary backstroke	Add the arm stroke to the breaststroke kick on the back. Practice the elementary backstroke standing in water about chest deep. ▪ Hang the arms down to the side.

			▪ Keeping the fingertips on the body, raise the hands UP to the armpits. ▪ Point the fingertips away from the body and extend the arms OUT to the side. Keep the arms level with the shoulders. ▪ Sweep the hands down TOGETHER to the side. When swimming elementary backstroke, the arms and legs begin and end simultaneously. Practice the elementary backstroke. ▪ Start with a back glide. ▪ Move the arms and legs simultaneously UP, OUT and TOGETHER. ▪ GLIDE in the streamline position with the arms at the side. ▪ Repeat.
11	5 minutes	Treading water	Treading water is the ability to remain in the same area in a vertical position in deep water keeping the head above water. Practice the arm motion while standing in water about chest deep or while floating on a foam noodle. ▪ Extend the arms forward and slightly wider than shoulder width. ▪ Relax and bend the elbows about half way. ▪ Position the hands with the palms down slightly under the surface. ▪ Turn the palms out some and sweep the hands out and down. ▪ Turn the palms inward some and sweep the hands back toward the original position. ▪ Repeat continuously.

			The leg motion is similar to the breaststroke kick without the legs ever coming together. The legs never extend straight in the wide (OUT) position or in the close together (IN) position. Practice the leg motion. Practice while floating on a foam noodle, sitting on the side of the pool with the legs hanging down, sitting in water about chest deep or supported by the instructor. ▪ Bend the knees UP and move the legs apart. This position is like sitting on a horse. ▪ Flex the ankles and move the legs OUT some. ▪ Point the toes down and forcefully move the legs IN some. As the feet move the water toward the center, the bottom of the feet should feel resistance of the water. ▪ Repeat continuously. Some people are more comfortable treading with an alternating leg motion. This is called a rotary kick or eggbeater. To practice a rotary kick: ▪ Follow the same instructions above. ▪ Alternate the legs UP, OUT, and IN one leg at time continuously. Practice treading water in water about shoulder deep. ▪ Lean forward slightly. ▪ Lift the feet off the bottom and simultaneously move the arms and legs. Move vigorously enough to keep the head above water and the body in a vertical position with relative comfort. ▪ Practice for five seconds at a time and

			increase the time with increased proficiency. ▪ When comfortable and proficient at treading in water about shoulder deep, practice treading in deep water.
12	5 minutes	Game	Retrieve sinking toys in deeper water. Place toys at the bottom in water as deep as can managed.

GOOD HABIT TIP: When swimming the front crawl, roll the body slightly, side to side from head to toe. This movement is called "body roll". Body roll is the element of the front crawl that helps the stroke remain efficient and smooth. It helps the efficiency of rotary breathing, the power and recovery of the arms and helps to keep the body straight, preventing it from bending and twisting.

Chapter 9 – Lesson 8

In Lesson 8 learners continue to practice the skills practiced and learned in Lessons 1, 2, 3, 4, 5, 6 and 7. By now, learners are swimmers because their swimming ability will have improved greatly. By continuing to practice, swimmers will gain strength and a greater level of comfort in the water.

LESSON 8 – 32 MINUTES 15 SECONDS			
#	TIME ESTIMATE	SKILLS	DESCRIPTION / INSTRUCTIONS
1	15 seconds	Jump in and swim back to the wall.	See Lessons 4 and 5, pages 35 and 37.
2	3 minutes	Front glide and flutter kick - with a kickboard - with or without assistance	See Lesson 1, page 13.
3	3 minutes	Back glide and flutter kick - with a kickboard - with or without assistance	See Lesson 2, page 21.
4	3 minutes	Back glide and breaststroke kick - with a kickboard - with or without assistance	See Lesson 5, page 38.
5	3 minutes	Front glide and breaststroke kick - with a kickboard - with or without assistance	See Lesson 5, page 39.
6	3 minutes	Front crawl - with rotary breathing	See Lesson 7, page 46.
7	3 minutes	Flutter kick on the back - with finning	See Lesson 3, page 26.
8	3 minutes	Elementary backstroke	See Lesson 7, page 47.
9	3 minutes	Survival float	See Lesson 6, page 43.
10	3 minutes	Treading water	See Lesson 7, page 48.
11	5 minutes	Game	Choose any game previously played.

I hope that learning to swim or teaching others to swim is as enjoyable and rewarding for you as it has been for me to present this material. Learning to swim well makes it possible for people to benefit from regular exercise and feeling safe in and around the water. When you are proficient at the skills learned and practiced in "Learn to Swim in 8 Lessons or Less," get the next book in this series "Learn to Swim Better in 8 Lessons or Less," available spring 2010. Breaststroke, backstroke, sidestroke, survival swimming and underwater swimming are learned and added to the routine. In addition drown proofing (swimming in clothes) is included in the lesson plans.

If you have any questions, need more guidance or would like to book me for lessons, send an email. My email address is bobby@bobbybroomeaquatics.com.

Always think "safety first" and have fun.

17294571R00033

Made in the USA
Charleston, SC
04 February 2013